W9-ALM-481

# The Census and America's People

★ ★ ★ ★ ★ ★ ★ ★ ★

### Analyzing Data Using Line Graphs and Tables

Natashya Wilson

# PowerMath™

The Rosen Publishing Group's
## PowerKids Press™
New York

Published in 2004 by The Rosen Publishing Group, Inc.
29 East 21st Street, New York, NY 10010

Book Design: Haley Wilson

Photo Credits: Cover, pp. 7, 29 (both), 30 © Bettmann/Corbis; pp. 4, 5, 19 © PhotoDisc; pp. 11, 15 © Corbis.

Library of Congress Cataloging-in-Publication Data

Wilson, Natashya.
  The census and America's people : analyzing data using line graphs and tables / Natashya Wilson.
        v. cm. — (PowerMath)
Includes index.
Contents: What is the census all about? — America 1790: the first census — The growth of a nation — Immigrants and the census — Minority report — Men, women, and children — America goes west — Looking toward the future.
  ISBN 0-8239-8990-9 (lib. bdg.)
  ISBN 0-8239-8903-8 (pbk.)
  6-pack ISBN: 0-8239-7431-6
  1. Statistics—Graphic methods—Juvenile literature. 2. United States—Census—Juvenile literature. [1. Statistics—Graphic methods. 2. United States—Census. 3. Graphic methods.] I. Title. II. Series.
  QA276.3.W58 2004
  001.4'226—dc21
                                        2003006001

Manufactured in the United States of America

# Contents

# What Is the Census All About?

A census is the counting of all the people in a population. In the United States of America, the U.S. Census Bureau counts the entire population of America once every 10 years. The census tells us more than just the number of people in the country. It also tells us the number of men, the number of women, and the number of people in different **minority** groups in America. These numbers are called **data**.

We can use tables and line graphs to organize information from the census and to **analyze** what it means. A table organizes data into columns and rows so that it is easy to read. A line graph organizes data to show changes over time. It can also compare the changes between 2 or more things over time. Often a line graph can be made from the data provided in a table.

A line graph has a line, or **axis**, that goes from left to right, and another axis that runs up and down. The left-to-right axis is called the X-axis. The up-and-down axis is called the Y-axis.

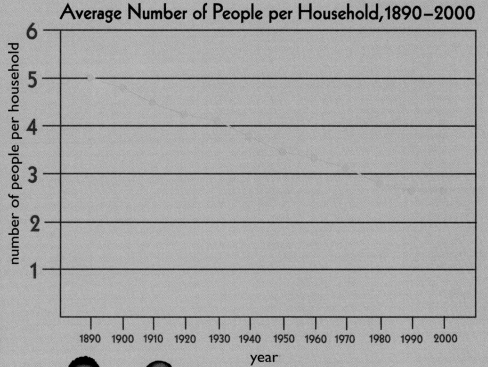

## Average Number of People per Household, 1890–2000

number of people per household

6

5

4

3

2

1

1890 1900 1910 1920 1930 1940 1950 1960 1970 1980 1990 2000

year

This line graph represents the changing size of the average American household from 1890 to 2000. Five people lived in an average household in 1890. In 2000, fewer than 3 people lived in an average household.

★ ★ ★ ★ ★ ★ ★ ★ ★ ★ ★ ★ ★ ★ ★ ★

America's early leaders wrote the rules for governing the United States at the Constitutional Convention in 1787. At this important meeting in Philadelphia, representatives from the newly formed states met to set up a government for the new nation. They came up with a special set of laws, now known as the Constitution.

According to the Constitution, the people of America have the right to choose the people who will become members of Congress. Congress makes new laws. It is made up of 2 groups called the Senate and the House of Representatives. Each state has 2 members in the Senate. The number of members each state has in the House of Representatives depends on each state's population. To make sure that each state has the right number of representatives, the government counts each state's population, and therefore the population of the whole United States, every 10 years. This is one reason why the census is so important!

At first, the Secretary of State was the government leader in charge of the census. Then the census became the responsibility of the **Department of the Interior**. Finally, the federal government created the U.S. Census Bureau in 1903. The U.S. Census Bureau is responsible for gathering census information and reporting population numbers. People can use census data to study how the population changes over time.

★ ★ ★ ★ ★ ★ ★ ★ ★ ★ ★ ★ ★ ★ ★ ★

In the 1930s, when this photograph was taken, people from the Census Bureau went from house to house asking questions about the people who lived there. Then, all the results were added up by hand!

# America 1790: The First Census

President George Washington signed the census into law on March 1, 1790. Secretary of State Thomas Jefferson was in charge of the census. The first count began on August 2, 1790. Seventeen U.S. **marshals** and their 600 helpers were given 9 months to visit every household in America and question the people who lived there. It took them 18 months to complete the census. The census takers often had to try to track down people who did not want to answer the census questions. Many people feared their taxes would be raised if they were counted.

The counts included the 13 states of New Hampshire, Massachusetts, Rhode Island, Connecticut, New York, New Jersey, Pennsylvania, Delaware, Maryland, Virginia, North Carolina, South Carolina, and Georgia. It also included the districts of Kentucky, Maine, and Vermont—which were not yet states—and the area known as the Southwest Territory.

**The first census asked for 6 pieces of
information from each household:**

1. Name of the head of the family
2. Number of free white males 16 and over
3. Number of free white males under 16
4. Number of free white females
5. Number of other free persons
6. Number of slaves

# Results of 1790 Census

| Group | Total |
|---|---|
| • Free white males 16 and older, including heads of families | 813,365 |
| • Free white males under 16 | 802,127 |
| • Free white females, including heads of families | 1,556,628 |
| • All other free persons | 59,511 |
| • Slaves | 697,697 |
| Total Population | 3,929,328 |

We can learn many things from this table. By adding up the first 3 numbers in the "Total" column, we can see that of the 3,929,328 people counted, 3,172,120 were white. "All other free persons" included free black people and Native Americans who paid taxes. Many Native Americans did not pay taxes, and so they were not counted in the census.

# The Growth of a Nation

Between 1790 and 1860, the population of the United States grew by about 35% every 10 years. The census showed that the population of the northern states was growing faster than the population of the southern states.

Look at the table on page 11. In 1860, about 11 million people lived in the southern states. Nearly 4 million were slaves. More than 19 million people lived in the North. Only about 115,000—or less than 1%—were slaves.

Growing disagreements about slavery between the industrial North and the agricultural South led to the terrible American Civil War, fought from 1861 to 1865. The 1860 census was the last to count slaves. After the Civil War ended, all the slaves were free.

From the first census until the census of 1870, blacks who were slaves were recorded as 1 person in the census records. However, slaves counted as only $\frac{3}{5}$ of a person when calculating the number of representatives to Congress. Native Americans were not counted separately until 1860. Before then, they were included in the "other free persons" category, and then only if they lived in the white community and paid taxes.

# Population, 1860

| Region | Total Population | Slaves |
|---|---|---|
| North | 19,690,984 | 114,966 |
| South | 11,133,361 | 3,838,765 |
| West | 618,976 | 29 |
| Total, U.S. | 31,443,321 | 3,953,760 |

How many slaves lived in the United States in 1860?
You can find the answer in the lower right corner of the table. Slaves made up about $\frac{1}{8}$ of the total U.S. population.

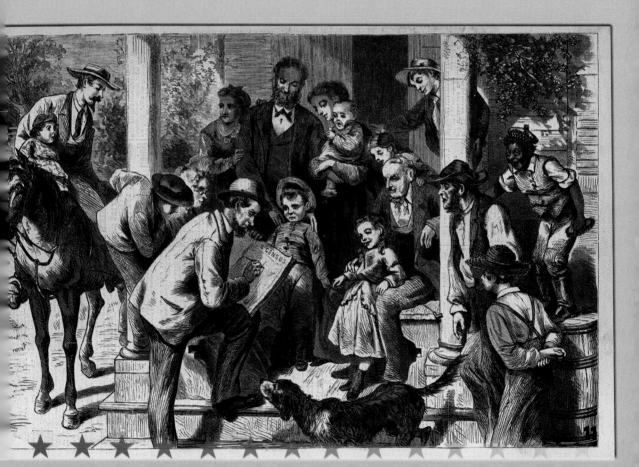

Between 1860 and 1920, America's population shifted from living in mostly rural areas to living in mostly **urban** places. More and more people were leaving the farms and the countryside to live in the city. By 1920, America's population had grown to more than 106 million. In 1970, the census showed that more Americans lived in the **suburbs** than in either the city or the country.

America's population has grown larger with every census. The slowest growth was between 1930 and 1940, during the **Great Depression**. Many people lost their jobs and their homes in the 1930s. However, because no census was taken between 1930 and 1940, no one knows exactly how many people were without jobs or homes. Since then, the Census Bureau has added more questions about housing and jobs to the census. The bureau also receives a monthly count of how many people have jobs and how many do not.

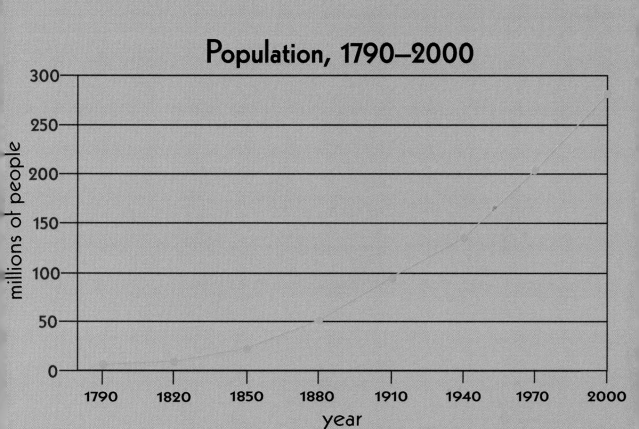

# Population, 1790–2000

By looking at this line graph, we can see that in the year 1880, there were about 50 million people in America. About how many people lived in America in 1970? The graph shows that there were about 200 million people living in America in 1970.

# Immigrants and the Census

Since 1607, America has been settled by **immigrants**. They first came in small groups. Soon, more and more people began arriving. At first, the United States encouraged immigration from Europe. More people coming to live in America meant that the cities and towns would grow and more jobs would be created. The government wanted America to become a large, strong country.

Millions of Irish and Germans moved to America in the 1840s and 1850s, driven away from their home countries by war or a lack of food or work. Although Asians were not counted in the census until 1860, many Asians came to America during the California Gold Rush, which began in 1848. Many other immigrants were Italians and Russian Jews who came to escape poverty and crime in their countries. Altogether, more than 47 million immigrants arrived in America between 1890 and 1930. Many immigrants came through Ellis Island. Ellis Island is a small island in New York Harbor where immigrants were counted and checked for illnesses before entering America.

The 1850 census was the first to count all the people in America who had been born in other countries. That year, about 2.3 million people had been born in other countries. In 2000, more than 28 million people in America had been born in other countries.

immigrants at Ellis Island in 1906

By the 1920s, many Americans began to fear that immigrants were taking jobs away from people who were born in America. Immigrants were not just coming from Europe, but from all over the world, and many Americans were uncomfortable with the languages and customs of these new immigrants. The American government greatly cut back on immigration beginning in the 1920s until about 1965, when new laws were passed allowing more immigrants to enter America.

In the 1970s, 1980s, and 1990s, another large group of immigrants arrived. These immigrants came mostly from Asia and Latin America. About 7 million Asians and 14 million Latin Americans came to America during these 3 decades. Many settled in the West, helping California to become the country's most populated state.

# Immigration, 1831–2000

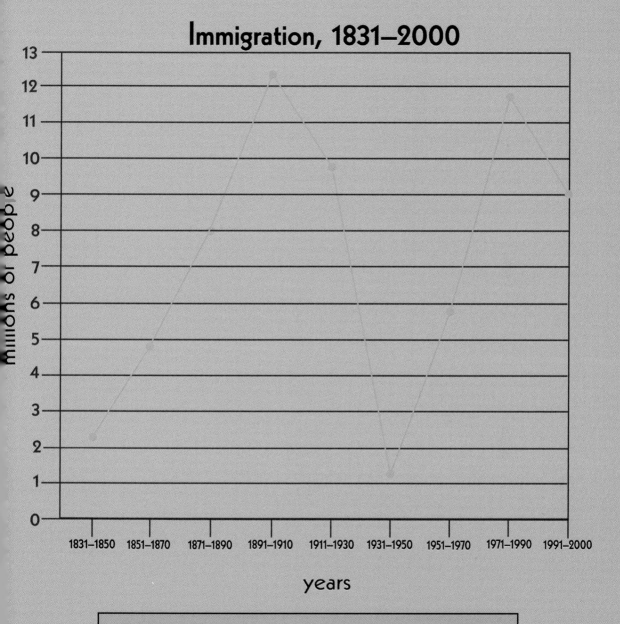

This line graph shows the number of immigrants who came to America between 1831 and 2000. By looking at the graph, you can tell that immigration was lowest between 1931 and 1950. The greatest number of people arrived between 1891 and 1910.

# Minority Report

Immigration has greatly changed the population of America. Many immigrants have come from minority groups. Minorities now make up about $\frac{1}{4}$ of America's population. The Census Bureau believes that by 2050, minorities may make up about $\frac{1}{2}$ of the population! Minority information is used to help decide voting districts and to find out if all people have equal opportunities for jobs and housing. It is also used to make or to change government programs that help minorities.

In 2000, for the first time ever, people were able to count themselves as part of more than one **racial** group. Most of America's population counted themselves as white. Nearly 7 million people described themselves as belonging to 2 or more races. Exactly 823 people reported that they belonged to 6 racial groups!

Hispanics slightly outnumbered blacks in the 2000 census. This was the first time blacks were not the nation's largest minority. The Asian community has also grown rapidly in recent years. The number of people of Asian origin in America more than doubled in the 1980s and 1990s.

Blacks are the only minorities who have been counted in every American census. They were the nation's largest minority group for 200 years. Asians and Native Americans (called "American Indians" in the census) were not counted as separate groups until 1860. The "other race" group became a choice in 1950.

In the 2000 census, people were also asked whether or not they considered themselves to be of Hispanic origin. This question was first asked in the 1940 census to a small sample of the population. It was not asked again until 1970! "Hispanic" is not a race. It indicates someone whose family came from a Spanish-speaking region, such as Mexico, Central or South America, or Puerto Rico. People who are Hispanic are counted in the census as a minority group.

This line graph compares the numbers of people in the 3 largest minority groups and the growth of the groups. By looking at this graph, you can see that about 13 million blacks were living in America in 1940. About 15 million Hispanics were living in America in 1980. The graph will also tell you that the U.S. populations of Hispanics and blacks in the year 2000 were about equal.

# Growth of the 3 Largest Minority Groups, 1800–2000

millions of people

year

☐ Black/African American ■ Hispanic/Latino ☐ Asian/Pacific Islander

# Men, Women, and Children

Questions on age and **gender** have been part of the census from the beginning. At first, this information was used to find out how many men were old enough to vote and to serve in the military. Because of this, men who were 16 or older were counted separately from younger males. Because women at the time could not vote or serve in the military, all women were counted in a single group. Today the numbers are used for many purposes, such as studies of the nation's health, the need for new schools, and how to best care for older people.

Census data shows us that today, men usually make more money than women. It also shows us that women live longer than men. It shows that about $\frac{1}{4}$ of the population is under age 18. About 20 million children will reach high-school age by 2005, a 20% increase from the 1990 census. More than 19 million children will be old enough to start elementary school in 2005, a 4% increase from 1990. This tells us that America will need more schools.

Today in the United States, about 14 babies for every 1,000 people are born each year. The number of male and female babies is about equal. However, there are more women than men in the U.S. population. This is partly because people today live longer than they did before 1950 and women usually live longer than men.

# Number of Men for Every 100 Women, 1900–2000

| Year | Women | Men |
|------|-------|-----|
| 1900 | 100 | 105 |
| 1910 | 100 | 106 |
| 1920 | 100 | 104 |
| 1930 | 100 | 103 |
| 1940 | 100 | 101 |
| 1950 | 100 | 99 |
| 1960 | 100 | 97 |
| 1970 | 100 | 95 |
| 1980 | 100 | 94 |
| 1990 | 100 | 95 |
| 2000 | 100 | 96 |

This table shows us that between 1900 and 2000, the number of men per 100 women was at its highest point in 1910. In 1980 it was at its lowest point. In 2000, the census counted 96 men per 100 women, 1 more than in 1990. The increase may have been because more men immigrated to America in the 1990s. The 2000 census may also have done a better job of counting men in minority groups than in 1990.

Better living conditions, better health care, and new medicines increased **life expectancy** during the 20th century. Life expectancy has grown longer for both men and women. In 1790, people could expect to live to be 35 years old. By 1900, life expectancy was 47 years. Today it is about 74 years for men and 80 years for women. The table on this page and the graph on page 25 both show the change in life expectancy for men and women from 1940 to 2000.

## Life Expectancy for Men and Women, 1940–2000

| Year | Men | Women |
|------|-----|-------|
| 1940 | 60.8 | 65.2 |
| 1950 | 65.6 | 71.1 |
| 1960 | 66.6 | 73.1 |
| 1970 | 67.1 | 74.7 |
| 1980 | 70.0 | 77.4 |
| 1990 | 71.8 | 78.8 |
| 2000 | 74.1 | 79.5 |

Women have a longer life expectancy than men. How much has life expectancy changed for women from 1940 to 2000? Subtract 65.2 from 79.5 to find your answer.

$$
\begin{array}{r}
79.5 \\
-65.2 \\
\hline
14.3
\end{array}
$$

In 2000, the census showed that women live an average of about 14 years longer than they did in 1940.

# Life Expectancy for Men and Women, 1940–2000

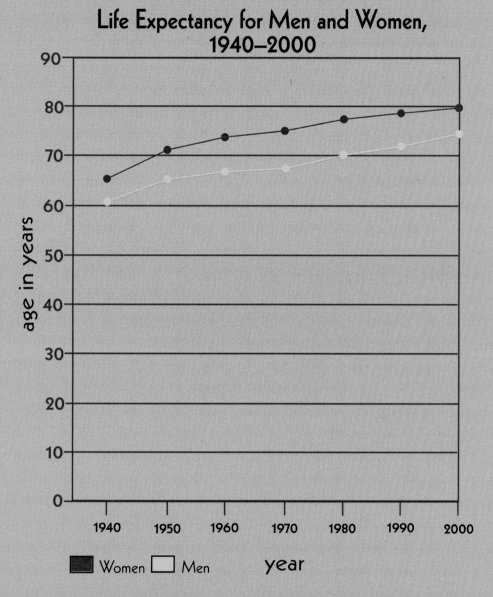

In 2000, almost 2 million people were less than 1 year old.
Exactly 1,388 were older than 110 years old!

# America Goes West

When U.S. marshals took the first census in 1790, most of the population lived near the East Coast. Since that time, Americans have moved west in larger and larger numbers, exploring and claiming territory until the 1840s, when America reached all the way to the West Coast.

As the country grew in size and population, the census also grew in the amount of information gathered. As more questions were added and more people had to be counted, the job of reporting all the information took longer and longer. The final results of the 1880 census were not fully known until 1887!

In the next century, America reached still farther west when Alaska and Hawaii became states in 1959. Although no new land has been added to America since then, the nation's population has grown rapidly, especially in the West. The population in California tripled between 1950 and 2000!

# Top 5 States in Population, 1900, 1950, 2000

## 1900

| Rank | State | Population |
|------|-------|-----------|
| 1 | New York | 7,268,894 |
| 2 | Pennsylvania | 6,302,115 |
| 3 | Illinois | 4,821,550 |
| 4 | Ohio | 4,157,545 |
| 5 | Missouri | 3,106,665 |

## 1950

| Rank | State | Population |
|------|-------|-----------|
| 1 | New York | 14,830,192 |
| 2 | California | 10,586,223 |
| 3 | Pennsylvania | 10,498,012 |
| 4 | Illinois | 8,712,176 |
| 5 | Ohio | 7,946,627 |

## 2000

| Rank | State | Population |
|------|-------|-----------|
| 1 | California | 33,871,648 |
| 2 | Texas | 20,851,820 |
| 3 | New York | 18,976,457 |
| 4 | Florida | 15,982,378 |
| 5 | Illinois | 12,419,293 |

These tables show which states had the most people in 1900, 1950, and 2000. You can see that New York had the largest population in 1900 and 1950. In 2000, California and Texas had more people. If you look at a map, you will see that both California and Texas are west of New York.

Until 1890, census workers counted all census results by hand. To make the job of counting the census information go faster, a better way of counting was needed. In 1881, a man named Herman Hollerith invented a machine that could count holes punched in cards. For the 1890 census, the census takers punched answers to the census questions into cards that the machine could read. This was a much faster and easier way to count the results of the census.

Herman Hollerith kept improving his counting machines. In 1896, he started his own company, the Tabulating Machine Company. In 1911, the Tabulating Machine Company and another company joined to form a new company. In 1924, this new company became International Business Machines, or IBM. Today, IBM is one of the largest computer manufacturers in the world.

This picture shows computer operators adding up the numbers of the 1954 census. The computer they are using is much larger than the computers of today!

Herman Hollerith

# Looking Toward the Future

The U.S. Census Bureau uses data to try to estimate what might happen in America's future. These estimates are made based on what has happened in the past and how much things such as birthrate, life expectancy, and immigration have changed over time.

The Census Bureau uses tables and graphs to organize and study census information, just as you have done in this book. The data shown in these tables and graphs is used every day by census workers, schools, government leaders, health care workers, and many others. The U.S. Census Bureau will continue to gather information and help to plan for the future of America's growing population, which could be more than 1 billion people by the year 2100!

# Glossary

**analyze** (AA-nuhl-ize)  To study something very carefully.

**axis** (AK-suhs)  Either of the lines that form the left side and bottom of a graph and tell what is being measured.

**data** (DAY-tuh)  Information.

**Department of the Interior** (dih-PAHRT-muhnt UV THEE in-TEER-ee-uhr)  The part of the federal government that is responsible for conserving the country's natural resources.

**gender** (JEN-dur)  Male or female.

**Great Depression** (GRAYT dih-PREH-shun)  A period of history that lasted from 1929 until 1942. Banks and businesses lost money, and millions of people lost their jobs.

**immigrant** (IH-muh-grunt)  A person who moves to a new country from another country.

**life expectancy** (LYF ik-SPEK-tun-see)  The average length of a person's life.

**marshal** (MAR-shul)  A type of policeman.

**minority** (muh-NOHR-uh-tee)  A part of the population that is different from the larger part of the population.

**racial** (RAY-shul)  Having to do with race.

**suburb** (SUH-burb)  A small community that is close to a big city.

**urban** (UHR-bun)  Having to do with a city.

# Index